The Importance of Reading Fluency

by Gerald Tindal, Ph.D.

Struggling readers, in general, lack fluency. Therefore, attention to fluency instruction should be a major component of any reading program.

As defined by the National Reading Panel (2000), fluency is "reading text with speed, accuracy, and proper expression." Fluent readers are like musicians or athletes who no longer have to "think" about a behavior; they "just do it." A fluent reader moves over the words, sequencing them effortlessly, providing appropriate intonation, and integrating the punctuation. Fluent reading is easily discerned by the reader's audience.

The importance of reading fluency cannot be underestimated, or its relevance doubted. Comprehension improves when students read quickly, accurately, and smoothly. Jay Samuels, of the University of Minnesota, used the term *automaticity* to describe the relationship between decoding and comprehension. Basically, when students become fluent, decoding is automatic and no cognitive effort is needed to read; the result is a nearly total focus on comprehension.

Additionally, there are some major side benefits of fluency instruction. As students become more fluent readers, they can begin to command their own learning and participate more broadly in the language community. With reading fluency comes greater awareness of the world and opportunity to interact with others, allowing students to help each other practice, rehearse for performances, and share their skills with an audience.

Enjoy helping your students move toward reading fluency!

Dr. Tindal is the Castle-McIntosh-Knight Professor of Education at the University of Oregon in Eugene, Oregon.

Teaching Fluency

In order for students to become fluent readers, they need to have oral reading **modeled** for them; they need repeated oral reading **practice**; and they benefit greatly from **performing** their oral reading.

MODELING ORAL READING

Use the overhead transparencies in this book to demonstrate various qualities of fluent oral reading: rate, phrasing, and intonation. (More about using the transparencies appears on page 4.)

Rate
Explain to students that oral reading rate varies depending on the type of selection being read.

- A faster rate is appropriate for lighthearted pieces such as riddles, jokes, tongue twisters, and limericks.

- A slower rate will better convey meaning when reading nonfiction selections or folk tales and myths.

- Readers' Theater should be read at a rate that corresponds with spoken dialogue.

Phrasing
Explain the importance of reading in phrases, rather than word by word. Use the transparencies to demonstrate how to divide text into meaningful chunks (see page 4).

Intonation
Intonation is the distinctive tone of voice that conveys meaning. Guide students to scan ahead for punctuation that signals appropriate intonation.

- A question mark signals the reader to end the sentence with a slightly higher voice.

- An exclamation mark indicates words that should be read with strong feeling.

- Words in quotation marks should be read as if they are being spoken.

Building Fluency • EMC 3345 • © Evan-Moor Corp.

PRACTICING ORAL READING

Keep fluency practice fun and interesting by using a variety of techniques, such as those explained below. Older students may have their own ideas about ways to enliven practice.

Choral Reading

Choral reading is simply reading in unison. Enliven your fluency practice by trying a number of approaches to choral reading throughout the year:

- Refrain reading—one student reads most of the piece and the rest of the class reads repeated sections.

- Antiphonal reading—small groups of students are each assigned a different section of text. One group reads its part, and a different group reads another part, such as the chorus or refrain. This technique is effective with chants, songs, and poems.

- Radio reading—small groups of four to six students are assigned a passage of text. Each student reads a part of the passage in the proper order. This technique is perfect for speeches, nonfiction, and tales, myths, and legends.

- Call and response—one student reads part of a joke or riddle, for example, and the whole group responds by reading the punch line or answer.

- Cumulative—one child or small group begins the reading and is sequentially joined by one or more readers until the entire class is reading.

Partner Reading

In partner reading, one student reads a line or a part, and the partner reads the next line or part.

Echo Reading

In echo reading, a proficient reader is paired with a less proficient reader. The better reader reads one sentence or phrase. The other reader echoes back, following along with a finger.

PERFORMING ORAL READING

A performance celebrates the fluency achieved by daily practice. Friday afternoons are a perfect time for your readers to strut their stuff. Invite a buddy class or someone special, such as the principal, to share in the fun!

Using the Transparencies

The Transparencies

Twenty selections from this book are provided on transparencies to assist you in modeling appropriate rate, phrasing, and intonation for students. These selections are also indicated in the Table of Contents for each section of the book.

Demonstrating Phrasing on the Transparencies

Fluent readers divide text into meaningful "chunks," rather than reading word by word. For example, when a fluent reader reads the sentence "Slue-Foot Sue / was one of the greatest ladies / of the Texas frontier," he or she would automatically pause as indicated by the slash marks.

Demonstrate how to cluster words together by making slash marks (/) with a marking pen on a chosen transparency. Read the selection to the students, and then read chorally as a group. Practice several times, with and without the slash marks.

Starting below and continuing through page 6, you will find reductions of the transparency selections showing suggested markings for phrasing.

Page 16 **Page 17** **Page 19**

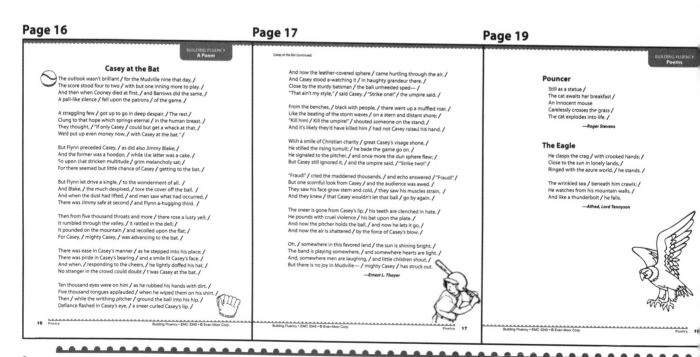

Page 16 — Casey at the Bat (A Poem)

The outlook wasn't brilliant / for the Mudville nine that day, /
The score stood four to two / with but one inning more to play. /
And then when Cooney died at first, / and Barrows did the same, /
A pall-like silence / fell upon the patrons / of the game. /

A straggling few / got up to go in deep despair. / The rest /
Clung to that hope which springs eternal / in the human breast. /
They thought, / "If only Casey / could but get a whack at that. /
We'd put up even money now, / with Casey at the bat." /

But Flynn preceded Casey, / as did also Jimmy Blake; /
And the former was a hoodoo, / while the latter was a cake. /
So upon that stricken multitude / grim melancholy sat; /
For there seemed but little chance of Casey / getting to the bat. /

But Flynn let drive a single, / to the wonderment of all. /
And Blake, / the much despised, / tore the cover off the ball. /
And when the dust had lifted, / and men saw what had occurred, /
There was Jimmy safe at second / and Flynn a-hugging third. /

Then from five thousand throats and more / there rose a lusty yell; /
It rumbled through the valley, / it rattled in the dell; /
It pounded on the mountain / and recoiled upon the flat; /
For Casey, / mighty Casey, / was advancing to the bat. /

There was ease in Casey's manner / as he stepped into his place; /
There was pride in Casey's bearing / and a smile lit Casey's face. /
And when, / responding to the cheers, / he lightly doffed his hat, /
No stranger in the crowd could doubt / t'was Casey at the bat. /

Ten thousand eyes were on him / as he rubbed his hands with dirt. /
Five thousand tongues applauded / when he wiped them on his shirt. /
Then / while the writhing pitcher / ground the ball into his hip, /
Defiance flashed in Casey's eye, / a sneer curled Casey's lip. /

Page 17 — Casey at the Bat (continued)

And now the leather-covered sphere / came hurtling through the air, /
And Casey stood a-watching it / in haughty grandeur there. /
Close by the sturdy batsman / the ball unheeded sped— /
"That ain't my style," / said Casey. / "Strike one!" / the umpire said. /

From the benches, / black with people, / there went up a muffled roar, /
Like the beating of the storm waves / on a stern and distant shore; /
"Kill him! / Kill the umpire!" / shouted someone on the stand; /
And it's likely they'd have killed him / had not Casey raised his hand. /

With a smile of Christian charity / great Casey's visage shone, /
He stilled the rising tumult; / he bade the game go on. /
He signaled to the pitcher, / and once more the dun sphere flew; /
But Casey still ignored it, / and the umpire said, / "Strike two!" /

"Fraud!" / cried the maddened thousands, / and echo answered / "Fraud!" /
But one scornful look from Casey / and the audience was awed. /
They saw his face grow stern and cold, / they saw his muscles strain, /
And they knew / that Casey wouldn't let that ball / go by again. /

The sneer is gone from Casey's lip, / his teeth are clenched in hate. /
He pounds with cruel violence / his bat upon the plate. /
And now the pitcher holds the ball, / and now he lets it go, /
And now the air is shattered / by the force of Casey's blow. /

Oh, / somewhere in this favored land / the sun is shining bright. /
The band is playing somewhere, / and somewhere hearts are light. /
And, somewhere men are laughing, / and little children shout, /
But there is no joy in Mudville— / mighty Casey / has struck out. /

—Ernest L. Thayer

Page 19 — Poems

Pouncer

Still as a statue /
The cat awaits her breakfast /
An innocent mouse
Carelessly crosses the grass /
The cat explodes into life. /

—Roger Stevens

The Eagle

He clasps the crag / with crooked hands; /
Close to the sun in lonely lands, /
Ringed with the azure world, / he stands. /

The wrinkled sea / beneath him crawls; /
He watches from his mountain walls, /
And like a thunderbolt / he falls. /

—Alfred, Lord Tennyson

Building Fluency • EMC 3345 • © Evan-Moor Corp.

Building Fluency • EMC 3345 • © Evan-Moor Corp.

Page 25

BUILDING FLUENCY
A Poem

Windy Nights

Whenever the moon and stars are set, /
Whenever the wind is high, /
All night long / in the dark and wet, /
A man goes riding by. /
Late in the night / when the fires are out, /
Why does he gallop / and gallop about? /

Whenever the trees are crying aloud, /
And the ships are tossed at sea, /
By, on the highway, / low and loud, /
By at the gallop goes he. /
By at the gallop he goes, / and then /
By he comes back / at the gallop again.

—*Robert Louis Stevenson*

Building Fluency • EMC 3345 • © Evan-Moor Corp.   Poetry   25

Page 26

BUILDING FLUENCY
A Poem

O Captain! My Captain!

O Captain! / my Captain! / our fearful trip is done, /
The ship has weather'd every rack, / the prize we sought is won, /
The port is near, / the bells I hear, / the people all exulting, /
While follow eyes the steady keel, / the vessel grim and daring; /
    But O heart! / heart! / heart! /
      O the bleeding drops of red, /
        Where on the deck my Captain lies, /
          Fallen / cold and dead. /

O Captain! / my Captain! / rise up / and hear the bells; /
Rise up— / for you the flag is flung / —for you the bugle trills, /
For you / bouquets and ribbon'd wreaths / —for you / the shores crowding, /
For you they call, / the swaying mass, / their eager faces turning; /
    Here, Captain! / dear father! /
      This arm beneath your head! /
        It is some dream that on the deck /
          You've fallen / cold and dead. /

My Captain does not answer, / his lips are pale and still, /
My father does not feel my arm, / he has no pulse nor will; /
The ship is anchor'd / safe and sound, / its voyage closed and done, /
From fearful trip the victor ship / comes in with object won; /
    Exult, O shores! / and ring, O bells! /
      But I, / with mournful tread, /
        Walk the deck my Captain lies, /
          Fallen / cold and dead.

—*Walt Whitman*

Note: Walt Whitman wrote this poem following the assassination of Abraham Lincoln in 1865.

26   Poetry   Building Fluency • EMC 3345 • © Evan-Moor Corp.

Page 29

BUILDING FLUENCY
Riddles

Out of This World

What kind of songs / do planets like to sing? /

    (Nep-tunes!)

How did the astronaut / serve dinner / in outer space? /

    (On flying saucers!)

Where do astronauts / leave their spaceships? /

    (At parking meteors!)

How do you get a baby astronaut / to sleep? /

    (You rock it!)

Building Fluency • EMC 3345 • © Evan-Moor Corp.   Riddles, Jokes, Tongue Twisters, and Rhymes   29

Page 31

BUILDING FLUENCY
Knock Knock Jokes

Dozen

Knock, knock. /
Who's there? /
Dozen! /
Dozen who? /
Dozen anybody / want to play with me? /

Ben

Knock, knock. /
Who's there? /
Ben. /
Ben who? /
Ben knocking on the door / all afternoon! /

Arthur

Knock, knock. /
Who's there? /
Arthur. /
Arthur who? /
Arthur more cookies / in the jar? /

Building Fluency • EMC 3345 • © Evan-Moor Corp.   Riddles, Jokes, Tongue Twisters, and Rhymes   31

Page 33

BUILDING FLUENCY
Jokes

School Jokes

Father: How are your grades, / son? /
Son: Under water, / Dad. /
Father: Under water? / What do you mean? /
Son: They're below C level. /

Smart student: I'm taking French, / Spanish, / and algebra / this year. /
Less smart student: Okay. / Let me hear you say "good evening" / in algebra. /

Student: But / I don't think I deserve a zero / on this exam. /
Teacher: Neither do I, / but it's the lowest mark / I can give you.

Building Fluency • EMC 3345 • © Evan-Moor Corp.   Riddles, Jokes, Tongue Twisters, and Rhymes   33

Page 37

BUILDING FLUENCY
Rhymes

Little Miss Tuckett

Little Miss Tuckett /
Sat on a bucket, /
Eating some peaches and cream. /
There came a grasshopper /
And tried hard to stop her, /
But she said, "Go away, / or I'll scream."

—*Anonymous*

Twinkle, Twinkle, Little Bat

Twinkle, twinkle, / little bat! /
How I wonder / what you're at! /
Up above the world you fly, /
Like a tea tray / in the sky.

—*Lewis Carroll*

Note: These rhymes imitate the style of two familiar nursery rhymes. Do you know which ones?

Building Fluency • EMC 3345 • © Evan-Moor Corp.   Riddles, Jokes, Tongue Twisters, and Rhymes   37

Page 39

BUILDING FLUENCY
Nonfiction

Declaration of Independence

When in the Course of human events / it becomes necessary for one people / to dissolve the political bands / which have connected them with another / and to assume among the powers of the earth, / the separate and equal station / to which the Laws of Nature / and of Nature's God / entitle them, / a decent respect to the opinions of mankind / requires that they should declare the causes / which impel them to the separation. /

We hold these truths to be self-evident, / that all men are created equal, / that they are endowed by their Creator / with certain unalienable Rights, / that among these are Life, / Liberty / and the pursuit of Happiness. / —That to secure these rights, / Governments are instituted among Men, / deriving their just powers / from the consent of the governed, / — That whenever any Form of Government / becomes destructive of these ends, / it is the Right of the People / to alter or to abolish it, / and to institute new Government, / laying its foundation on such principles / and organizing its powers in such form, / as to them shall seem most likely / to effect their Safety and Happiness.

Building Fluency • EMC 3345 • © Evan-Moor Corp.   Nonfiction   39

Page 43

BUILDING FLUENCY
A Speech

The Gettysburg Address
Abraham Lincoln

Fourscore and seven years ago / our fathers brought forth on this continent, / a new nation, / conceived in Liberty, / and dedicated to the proposition / that all men are created equal. /

Now we are engaged in a great civil war, / testing whether that nation, / or any nation / so conceived and so dedicated, / can long endure. / We are met on a great battlefield of that war. / We have come to dedicate a portion of that field, / as a final resting place / for those who here gave their lives that this nation might live. / It is altogether fitting and proper / that we should do this. /

But, in a larger sense, / we cannot dedicate / —we cannot consecrate / —we cannot hallow / —this ground. / The brave men, / living and dead, / who struggled here, / have consecrated it, far above our poor power to add or detract. / The world will little note, / nor long remember / what we say here, / but it can never forget / what they did here. / It is for us the living, rather, / to be dedicated here to the unfinished work / which they who fought here / have thus far so nobly advanced. / It is rather for us / to be here dedicated / to the great task remaining before us / —that from these honored dead / we take increased devotion / to that cause for which they gave the last full measure of devotion / —that we here highly resolve / that these dead shall not have died in vain / —that this nation, / under God, / shall have a new birth of freedom / —and that government of the people, / by the people, / for the people, / shall not perish from the earth.

Building Fluency • EMC 3345 • © Evan-Moor Corp.   Nonfiction   43

Page 48

BUILDING FLUENCY
Nonfiction

Antarctic Expedition

Ernest Shackleton / wanted to be the first explorer / to reach the South Pole. / It was Roald Amundsen, / however, / who claimed that honor / in 1911. / Disappointed, / Shackleton announced he would be the first explorer / to cross the entire Antarctic continent / —on foot! /

In August 1914, / Shackleton's ship *Endurance* / set sail from England. / After a stopover on South Georgia Island, / the *Endurance* headed south / and in January / entered the pack ice of the Weddell Sea. / The ship became completely trapped in an ice floe. / Huge blocks of ice crushed the sides of the ship, / and it sprung leaks. / Shackleton ordered the crew to abandon ship. / On November 21, 1915, / the crew watched the *Endurance* sink. / With three lifeboats / and limited supplies, / they were trapped hundreds of miles from land. /

Over the next five months, / Shackleton's crew lived on an ice floe. / Supplies ran out, / and blizzards raged on. / In April, / the ice began to break apart. / The lifeboats were launched. / Shackleton / knew the crew could not make it 700 miles / (1,122 km) / to South Georgia Island. / So they traveled to nearby Elephant Island instead. /

Elephant Island was a deserted wasteland. / The crew ate seals / and sucked on ice to survive. / Knowing his crew would not last long, / Shackleton made a difficult decision. / He / and five of his crew / would travel to South Georgia Island to get help. / He would leave twenty-two men behind. /

After seventeen treacherous days at sea, / Shackleton's crew reached the island / where they found help. / Fishermen helped get a boat for Shackleton. / But because of rough seas, / it took three months, / and four attempts, / to save all his crew on Elephant Island. /

In 1919, / Shackleton wrote about this amazing survival story / in a book entitled *South*.

48   Nonfiction   Building Fluency • EMC 3345 • © Evan-Moor Corp.

Building Fluency • EMC 3345 • © Evan-Moor Corp.

5

How to Build a Sand Castle

Building a sand castle / can be tricky. / If you dig a hole too close to the shoreline, / the castle may get washed out by waves. / If you are too far from the shore, / you will have to dig a very deep hole / in order to reach wet sand. / However, / for an almost perfect sand castle, / just follow the guidelines below. /

After choosing a good spot, / dig a hole / and place the scooped-out sand next to it. / Fill a bucket with seawater / and keep it next to your hole. / You are now ready / to start building your sand castle. /

Start by using moist sand / to make a flat, / even base for your castle. / Next, / use more of this sand / to build layers. / Think of how a grand, / layered wedding cake is stacked / with each layer getting smaller / as it reaches the top. / The easiest way to do this / is to sprinkle handfuls of sand / onto the base / and then gently flatten them / and mold them into a circular shape. / Each layer / should have a smaller circumference / than the previous one. / Use wet sand / to even out and smooth the tower layers. /

Finally, / you are ready to build the walls. / Use your bucket of seawater / to wet some sand. / Grab a handful of sand / and flatten it between your palms. / Use your hands to shape it into a brick / or block. / Next, / place the sand brick about six inches away from the tower. / Make more sand bricks, / and place them side by side, / creating a circle around the tower. / Now, / stand back / and admire your sand castle.

Bike Helmets Are Cool!

There are 28 million children, / ages 5 to 14, / who ride bicycles in this country. / Riding bicycles is fun / and good exercise / when you ride safely. / Unfortunately, / thousands of children / are disabled or die each year / as a result of bike accidents. / Experts / say wearing one piece of equipment / —a helmet / —can help save children. /

Today's bike helmets / are lightweight and comfortable. / A safe helmet / has a Consumer Product Safety Commission sticker inside. / This means it has been tested for safety. / But if a helmet has been in a crash, / it should be replaced. / Damaged helmets / lose their ability to absorb shock. /

Wearing bike helmets / saves lives. / But estimates show / that only about 15 to 25 percent of children who ride bikes / wear a helmet. / Children give excuses for not wearing a helmet. / Some say it's uncomfortable. / Problems occur when children wear helmets that are too small / or too big. / Children should not borrow other people's helmets. / The helmets need to fit just right. /

Some children / think it isn't cool / to wear bike helmets. / But you definitely won't look cool / if you crash and do damage to your body. / Studies show / that 90 percent of deaths due to head injuries / could be prevented / by wearing helmets. / Adding fluorescent, / reflective stickers to helmets / will make them look cooler. /

You probably think little kids get into more accidents. / The truth is / that boys between the ages of 10 and 14 / are more likely to be injured / or even killed / in bike accidents. /

Some people think they don't need to wear helmets / because they're riding close to home. / Studies show that most bike crashes / occur within one mile of home. / About 75 percent of child bike-accident deaths / occur where driveways, / alleys, / and streets intersect. /

Now you know the facts. / And yes, / it *is* cool to ride your bike safely!

How Butterflies Came to Be

Long, long ago, / when the Earth was very new, / Elder Brother walked around / to enjoy the beauty. / He gazed at the children playing. / Everywh on Earth, / they were playing joyfully. /

Elder Brother appreciated the children's happiness. / He saw how they loved the soft green grass, / the colors of flowers, / the sweet songs of birds and the soft rain. / He saw how the children loved the bright leaves / that fall from the trees / and fly around in the breeze. /

As he watched, / Elder Brother started to worry. / He thought, / "This joy may fly away some day, / and these children will be sad. / They might get sick / or be hungry. / They might get cold in the snow, / or be blown about harsh winds." /

Then Elder Brother / had a brainstorm / that made him happy again. / H picked up a big deerskin bag / and filled it with flowers and red and yellow leaves. / He added some blue feathers of the jaybird, / some blades of gree grass, / and some golden corn kernels. / He dropped in a handful of sunshine. / At the very last minute, / he threw in some bird songs. / Then Elder Brother / grasped the top of the bag in his large hands / and shook it many times / so that everything was mixed together. /

When he had mixed everything, / Elder Brother called to the children, / "Now come here / and open this bag!" /

When the bag was opened, / out fluttered thousands of shiny, / airy, / colorful creatures with wings. / They were the colors of all things on Earth, / and each creature sang a different song. /

The children laughed / and clapped with joy / as they chased the wonderful creatures. / "What are they? / What are they?" / the children shouted.

How Butterflies Came to Be (continued)

"These are my gift to you," / said Elder Brother. / "They are called butterflies. / If sad times come, / the sight of butterflies / may cheer you up. / On cold, stormy days / when the rain beats down, / the memory of butterflies / will warm your heart." /

But the birds / were not as happy as the children were. /

"Elder Brother," / the birds squawked, / "at the very beginning of the world, / colors were given to all living things. / Songs were given only to us birds. / We don't think it's fair / that these new creatures / should have our songs!" /

Elder Brother thought it over. / Then he replied, / "Birds, you are right. / Your songs are special, / and they should belong only to you." /

And that is how it is / to this very day. / The butterflies dance and fly / and make the children happy. / But they are silent. / Only the birds can sing.

Toads and Diamonds

Characters

Narrator 1	Narrator 2
Narrator 3	Regina
Mother	Old Woman
Princess	Bethany

Narrator 1: Once upon a time, / there lived a woman and her two daughters. / The elder daughter, / Regina, / and her mother were much alike. / Both were disagreeable and proud / and had never a kind word to say to anybody. /

Narrator 2: The younger daughter, / Bethany, / on the other hand, / had a sweet temper and a kind heart, / which showed in her lovely face. /

Narrator 3: The mother was partial to Regina, / of course, / because they were kindred spirits. / She was nasty to Bethany / and made her do all the scullery work. /

Mother: Bethany, / take this pitcher and go down to the spring. / And hurry up about it! / Your sister wants a cool drink. / Now go! /

Bethany: Yes, mother. / I will gladly fetch the water. /

Narrator 1: Now, the spring was two miles away, / and the day was unpleasantly warm. / But Bethany picked up the pitcher / and set out. /

Narrator 2: She was just filling her pitcher at the spring / when a ragged old woman / shuffled out of the woods. /

Old Woman: Girl, / I am weary and thirsty. / Do let me have a drink of cool water. /

Bethany: Of course. / Let me help you. /

Narrator 3: And Bethany held the cool pitcher / to the old woman's lips / while she drank her fill. /

Old Woman: I thank you for your kindness and good manners. / I give you a gift: / For every word you speak, / a diamond or ruby shall fall from your lips. /

Narrator 1: The old woman, / who was really a fairy in disguise, / limped back into the woods, / humming a tune / and leaving Bethany to refill her pitcher / and hurry home. /

Mother: Where have you been, / you lazy girl? / Can't you see that your sister is fainting / for lack of water? /

Bethany: I beg your pardon, Mother. /

Narrator 2: At these words, / two bright diamonds and three perfect rubies / fell from Bethany's lips / and dropped to the floor. /

Mother: What sort of trick is this? /

Bethany: It is no trick, Mother. / It happened at the spring. /

Narrator 3: And Bethany told her mother what had transpired, / while rubies and diamonds / gathered in heaps about her feet. /

Mother: Regina, / come here this minute! / Your sister is breathing riches. / You, too, must have this gift. / Run quickly now. / Go to the spring. / If an old woman asks for a drink, / give it to her. / And mind your manners. / Oh, / the riches you shall have, my love. / Hurry! /

Regina: Are you serious, Mother? / Surely you don't expect me to walk all the way to the spring / in this heat! / I shall ruin my slippers! /

Mother: Stop your grousing! / I'll ruin more than your slippers if you don't go! / Now, get! /

Narrator 1: Regina took her mother's finest filigreed pitcher from the cupboard / and flounced out of the house. /

Narrator 2: As soon as Regina arrived at the spring, / she saw a princess / in a gossamer gown / emerge from the woods. / Of course, / this was actually the same fairy, / appearing in a different form. /

Princess: Good day, young lady. / Would you kindly draw me a pitcher of water? /

Regina: Do you think I am a serving girl? / Get your own drink! /

Princess: My, / but you are disagreeable. / But though you will not oblige me with a drink / still I will give you a gift. /

Narrator 3: At the mention of gifts, / Regina's eyes lit up / and her contemptuous expression / changed to an expectant smile. /

Princess: This is your gift: / For every word you speak, / a toad or snake / shall fall from your lips. /

Narrator 1: And the princess / walked calmly away, / leaving Regina in abject tears. / When Regina at last gathered herself / and returned home, / her mother met her at the door. /

Mother: Why do you look so downcast, / my darling? /

Regina: Oh, Mother! / What a disaster! /

Narrator 2: As Regina spoke, / three lumpy toads and two green snakes / slithered from her lips / while her mother looked on in horror. /

Narrator 3: As the years passed, / Regina learned / that it was best for her to remain silent, / and so the house was more peaceful than it had ever been before. /

Narrator 1: But Bethany, / because of her good and generous nature, / sang all the day / and thus provided her mother and sister with all that they needed / and much that they wanted. /

Narrator 2: And the moral of the story? /

Narrator 3: Well, / that's for you to decide.

Love That Chocolate!

Chocolate comes from the seeds of the tropical cacao tree.	10
When chocolate is harvested, it doesn't have the same sweet	20
flavor you discover when you bite into a chocolate chip cookie.	31
A lot of work is needed to get that yummy chocolate taste.	43
The fruit of a cacao tree grows in a strange way. Football-shaped	55
pods grow from the trunk, not from the branches of the tree,	67
like apples do. It takes five to six months for the pods to change	81
from green to a ripe purple color. Then they are picked and cut	94
open.	95
Inside each pod are 20 to 40 white seeds, called beans, which	107
are about the size of almonds. The beans are surrounded by white	119
pulp. The pulp and beans are cut out of the pods and heated. The	133
heat turns the pulp into liquid, which is drained from the beans.	145
The beans are then dried. Drying turns them a dark chocolate color.	157
The smell from these beans is similar to the sweet odor of chocolate	170
in a candy bar, but the beans aren't chocolate quite yet.	181
The beans must be shipped to candy factories. Here the	191
chocolate beans are brushed clean, cooked, and crushed into	200
particles called nibs. The nibs are ground into a hard brown block	212
of cocoa. Different types of rich chocolate can be made from the	224
cocoa. Will it be made into baking chocolate? It could have sugar	236
added and become chocolate candy. Maybe it will flavor a truckload	247
of rocky road ice cream. What kind of chocolate would you like?	259

Assessing Oral Reading—
the One-Minute Probe

The one-minute probe is a very simple way to assess a student's oral reading fluency using norms established in an extensive study conducted by Jan Hasbrouck and Gerald Tindal in 2004.

On page 7 is a selection that may be used for a one-minute probe. There is a cumulative word count at the end of each line of text. You may also use other appropriate reading material that contains at least 194 words.

Preparation

- Reproduce two copies of the chosen selection, one for the student and one for the evaluator.

- You will need a watch with a second hand.

How to Conduct the Probe

1. Meet with the student individually.

2. Introduce the task to the student. Say, "Here is a reading selection about _____. I'd like you to read it to me at a speed that is right for you. Please read as accurately as you can. I will stop you after one minute."

3. Time the student for one minute as the student reads the selection aloud. If the student hesitates for 3 seconds, supply the word and tell the student to continue reading. On your copy, draw a line through any words that are supplied, omitted, or miscalled. At the end of a minute, make a slash mark after the last word the student read.

4. Count the number of miscalled words and subtract them from the total words read. This will give you the **words correct per minute (WCPM)**.

Recording Assessments

1. Find the grade level for the reading selection on the Oral Reading Fluency Data table on page 9.

2. In the correct "seasonal" column, locate the WCPM closest to the student's score.

3. Read across to the percentile column to get an approximate percentile norm for the student.

4. Chart the results on the Oral Reading Record Sheet on page 10. For an indication of growth in oral reading fluency, use this probe first in the fall (except for grade 1) and again in the winter and spring.

Building Fluency • EMC 3345 • © Evan-Moor Corp.

2005 Hasbrouck & Tindal
Oral Reading Fluency Data

Grade	Percentile	Fall (WCPM)	Winter (WCPM)	Spring (WCPM)
1	90		81	111
	75		47	82
	50		23	53
	25		12	28
	10		6	15
2	90	106	125	142
	75	79	100	117
	50	51	72	89
	25	25	42	61
	10	11	18	31
3	90	128	146	162
	75	99	120	137
	50	71	92	107
	25	44	62	78
	10	21	36	48
4	90	145	166	180
	75	119	139	152
	50	94	112	123
	25	68	87	98
	10	45	61	72
5	90	166	182	194
	75	139	156	168
	50	110	127	139
	25	85	99	109
	10	61	74	83
6	90	177	195	204
	75	153	167	177
	50	127	140	150
	25	98	111	122
	10	68	82	93
7	90	180	192	202
	75	156	165	177
	50	128	136	150
	25	102	109	123
	10	79	88	98
8	90	185	199	199
	75	161	173	177
	50	133	146	151
	25	106	115	124
	10	77	84	97

Adapted from Hasbrouck, J. E. & Tindal, G. (2006, April). Oral Reading Fluency Norms: A Valuable Assessment Tool for Reading Teachers. *The Reading Teacher,* 59(7). Copyright by the International Reading Association.

Oral Reading Record Sheet

Use this chart for recording the results of one-minute oral reading probes (see page 8).

Student Name	Fall (WCPM)	%	Winter (WCPM)	%	Spring (WCPM)	%

Building Fluency • EMC 3345 • © Evan-Moor Corp.

Poetry

* Transparency provided

Old Man from Peru

There was an old man from Peru
Who dreamed he was eating his shoe.
    In the midst of the night
    He awoke in a fright
And found it was perfectly true!

—Anonymous

Old Man in a Tree

There was an old man in a tree,
Whose whiskers were lovely to see;
    But the birds of the air
    Pluck'd them perfectly bare
To make themselves nests in that tree.

—Edward Lear

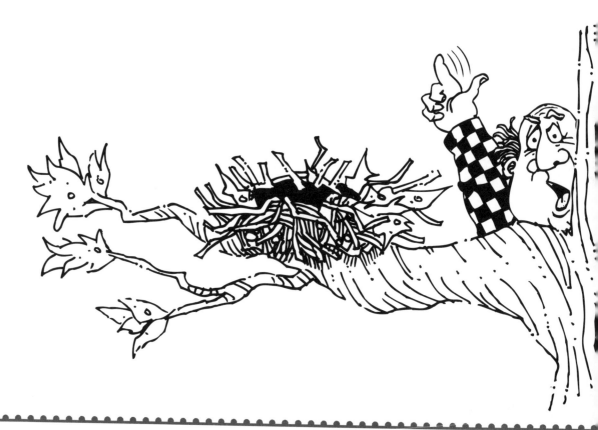

Name _____

Young Man of Bengal

There was a young man of Bengal
Who went to a fancy-dress ball.
   He went just for fun
   Dressed up as a bun—
And a dog ate him up in the hall.

              —Anonymous

Young Lady Whose Nose

There is a young lady whose nose,
Continually prospers and grows;
   When it grew out of sight,
   She exclaimed in a fright,
"Oh! Farewell to the end of my nose!"

             —Edward Lear

Birthday Blues

I was happy 'cause this year my birthday fell on Saturday
And I started making plans when it was still a month away.
I decided I would have a costume party and sleepover
So I made some invitations and invited my friends over.

It was gonna be the best, it was gonna be the greatest
We'd watch movies all night long and see who could stay up latest.
But on Friday afternoon when I came rushing home from school
My parents sat me down to say I'd broken several rules.

"Son, you didn't do your homework and you didn't do your chores.
You kept putting off the duties that you should have done before.
Your party has been cancelled—we called up all your friends.
You'd better get to work. This conversation's at an end."

I was boiling up like lava, let me tell you I was steaming.
I started yelling loud and moaning, groaning, even screaming.
I could feel my eyeballs aching and my stomach start to churn
But my parents wouldn't listen, they just said I had to learn.

So instead of getting presents, eating cake, and playing games
I've been washing, weeding, mowing and there's only me to blame.
If I'd just done this last Wednesday I'd be partying, and how!
So let this be a lesson—do your work and do it now.

—*Martha Cheney*

Building Fluency • EMC 3345 • © Evan-Moor Corp.

Name _____

My Shadow

I have a little shadow that goes in and out with me,
And what can be the use of him is more than I can see.
He is very, very like me from the heels up to the head;
And I see him jump before me, when I jump into my bed.

The funniest thing about him is the way he likes to grow—
Not at all like proper children, which is always very slow;
For he sometimes shoots up taller like an India-rubber ball,
And he sometimes gets so little that there's none of him at all.

He hasn't got a notion of how children ought to play,
And can only make a fool of me in every sort of way.
He stays so close beside he, he's a coward you can see;
I'd think shame to stick to nursie as that shadow sticks to me!

One morning very early, before the sun was up,
I rose and found the shining dew on every buttercup;
But my lazy little shadow, like an arrant sleepy-head
Had stayed at home behind me and was fast asleep in bed.

—*Robert Louis Stevenson*

Casey at the Bat

The outlook wasn't brilliant for the Mudville nine that day,
The score stood four to two with but one inning more to play.
And then when Cooney died at first, and Barrows did the same,
A pall-like silence fell upon the patrons of the game.

A straggling few got up to go in deep despair. The rest
Clung to that hope which springs eternal in the human breast.
They thought, "If only Casey could but get a whack at that.
We'd put up even money now, with Casey at the bat."

But Flynn preceded Casey, as did also Jimmy Blake;
And the former was a hoodoo, while the latter was a cake.
So upon that stricken multitude grim melancholy sat;
For there seemed but little chance of Casey getting to the bat.

But Flynn let drive a single, to the wonderment of all.
And Blake, the much despised, tore the cover off the ball.
And when the dust had lifted, and men saw what had occurred,
There was Jimmy safe at second and Flynn a-hugging third.

Then from five thousand throats and more there rose a lusty yell;
It rumbled through the valley, it rattled in the dell;
It pounded on the mountain and recoiled upon the flat;
For Casey, mighty Casey, was advancing to the bat.

There was ease in Casey's manner as he stepped into his place;
There was pride in Casey's bearing and a smile lit Casey's face.
And when, responding to the cheers, he lightly doffed his hat,
No stranger in the crowd could doubt t'was Casey at the bat.

Ten thousand eyes were on him as he rubbed his hands with dirt.
Five thousand tongues applauded when he wiped them on his shirt.
Then while the writhing pitcher ground the ball into his hip,
Defiance flashed in Casey's eye, a sneer curled Casey's lip.

And now the leather-covered sphere came hurtling through the air,
And Casey stood a-watching it in haughty grandeur there.
Close by the sturdy batsman the ball unheeded sped—
"That ain't my style," said Casey. "Strike one!" the umpire said.

From the benches, black with people, there went up a muffled roar,
Like the beating of the storm waves on a stern and distant shore;
"Kill him! Kill the umpire!" shouted someone on the stand;
And it's likely they'd have killed him had not Casey raised his hand.

With a smile of Christian charity great Casey's visage shone,
He stilled the rising tumult; he bade the game go on.
He signaled to the pitcher, and once more the dun sphere flew;
But Casey still ignored it, and the umpire said, "Strike two!"

"Fraud!" cried the maddened thousands, and echo answered "Fraud!"
But one scornful look from Casey and the audience was awed.
They saw his face grow stern and cold, they saw his muscles strain,
And they knew that Casey wouldn't let that ball go by again.

The sneer is gone from Casey's lip, his teeth are clenched in hate.
He pounds with cruel violence his bat upon the plate.
And now the pitcher holds the ball, and now he lets it go,
And now the air is shattered by the force of Casey's blow.

Oh, somewhere in this favored land the sun is shining bright.
The band is playing somewhere, and somewhere hearts are light.
And, somewhere men are laughing, and little children shout,
But there is no joy in Mudville—mighty Casey has struck out.

—**Ernest L. Thayer**

The New Colossus

Not like the brazen giant of Greek fame,
With conquering limbs astride from land to land;
Here at our sea-washed, sunset gates shall stand
A mighty woman with a torch, whose flame
Is the imprisoned lightning, and her name
Mother of Exiles. From her beacon-hand
Glows world-wide welcome; her mild eyes command
The air-bridged harbor that twin cities frame.
"Keep, ancient lands, your storied pomp!" cries she
With silent lips. "Give me your tired, your poor,
Your huddled masses yearning to breathe free,
The wretched refuse of your teeming shore.
Share these, the homeless, tempest-tost to me,
I lift my lamp beside the golden door!"

—*Emma Lazarus*

Note: *"The New Colossus," written in 1883, is engraved on
a plaque on the pedestal of the Statue of Liberty.*

Building Fluency • EMC 3345 • © Evan-Moor Corp.

Name _____

Pouncer

Still as a statue
The cat awaits her breakfast
An innocent mouse
Carelessly crosses the grass
The cat explodes into life.

—*Roger Stevens*

The Eagle

He clasps the crag with crooked hands;
Close to the sun in lonely lands,
Ringed with the azure world, he stands.

The wrinkled sea beneath him crawls;
He watches from his mountain walls,
And like a thunderbolt he falls.

—*Alfred, Lord Tennyson*

Name _____

Paul Revere's Ride

Listen, my children, and you shall hear
Of the midnight ride of Paul Revere,
On the eighteenth of April, in Seventy-five;
Hardly a man is now alive
Who remembers that famous day and year.

He said to his friend, "If the British march
By land or sea from the town to-night,
Hang a lantern aloft in the belfry arch
Of the North Church tower, as a signal light,—
One, if by land, and two, if by sea;
And I on the opposite shore will be,
Ready to ride and spread the alarm
Through every Middlesex village and farm,
For the country folk to be up and to arm."

Then he said "Good-night!" and with muffled oar
Silently rowed to the Charlestown shore,
Just as the moon rose over the bay,
Where swinging wide at her moorings lay
The Somerset, British man-of-war;
A phantom ship, with each mast and spar
Across the moon like a prison bar,
And a huge black hulk, that was magnified
By its own reflection in the tide.

Meanwhile, his friend through alley and street
Wanders and watches, with eager ears,
Till in the silence around him he hears
The muster of men at the barrack door,
The sound of arms, and the tramp of feet,
And the measured tread of the grenadiers,
Marching down to their boats on the shore.

Then he climbed the tower of the Old North Church,
By the wooden stairs, with stealthy tread,
To the belfry chamber overhead,
And startled the pigeons from their perch
On the sombre rafters, that round him made
Masses and moving shapes of shade,—
By the trembling ladder, steep and tall,
To the highest window in the wall,
Where he paused to listen and look down
A moment on the roofs of the town,
And the moonlight flowing over all.

Beneath, in the churchyard, lay the dead,
In their night encampment on the hill,
Wrapped in silence so deep and still
That he could hear, like a sentinel's tread,
The watchful night-wind, as it went
Creeping along from tent to tent,
And seeming to whisper, "All is well!"
A moment only he feels the spell
Of the place and the hour, and the secret dread
Of the lonely belfry and the dead;
For suddenly all his thoughts are bent
On a shadowy something far away,
Where the river widens to meet the bay,—
A line of black that bends and floats
On the rising tide like a bridge of boats.

Meanwhile, impatient to mount and ride,
Booted and spurred, with a heavy stride
On the opposite shore walked Paul Revere.
Now he patted his horse's side,
Now gazed on the landscape far and near,
Then, impetuous, stamped the earth,
And turned and tightened his saddle girth;
But mostly he watched with eager search
The belfry tower of the Old North Church,
As it rose above the graves on the hill,
Lonely and spectral and sombre and still.
And lo! as he looks, on the belfry's height
A glimmer, and then a gleam of light!
He springs to the saddle, the bridle he turns,
But lingers and gazes, till full on his sight
A second lamp in the belfry burns!

A hurry of hoofs in a village street,
A shape in the moonlight, a bulk in the dark,
And beneath, from the pebbles, in passing, a spark
Struck out by a steed flying fearless and fleet;
That was all! And yet, through the gloom and the light,
The fate of a nation was riding that night;
And the spark struck out by that steed, in his flight,
Kindled the land into flame with its heat.

He has left the village and mounted the steep,
And beneath him, tranquil and broad and deep,
Is the Mystic, meeting the ocean tides;
And under the alders that skirt its edge,
Now soft on the sand, now loud on the ledge,
Is heard the tramp of his steed as he rides.

Building Fluency • EMC 3345 • © Evan-Moor Corp.

It was twelve by the village clock
When he crossed the bridge into Medford town.
He heard the crowing of the cock,
And the barking of the farmer's dog,
And felt the damp of the river fog,
That rises after the sun goes down.

It was one by the village clock,
When he galloped into Lexington.
He saw the gilded weathercock
Swim in the moonlight as he passed,
And the meeting-house windows, black and bare,
Gaze at him with a spectral glare,
As if they already stood aghast
At the bloody work they would look upon.

It was two by the village clock,
When he came to the bridge in Concord town.
He heard the bleating of the flock,
And the twitter of birds among the trees,
And felt the breath of the morning breeze
Blowing over the meadow brown.
And one was safe and asleep in his bed
Who at the bridge would be first to fall,
Who that day would be lying dead,
Pierced by a British musket ball.

You know the rest. In the books you have read
How the British Regulars fired and fled,—
How the farmers gave them ball for ball,
From behind each fence and farm-yard wall,
Chasing the redcoats down the lane,
Then crossing the fields to emerge again
Under the trees at the turn of the road,
And only pausing to fire and load.

So through the night rode Paul Revere;
And so through the night went his cry of alarm
To every Middlesex village and farm,—
A cry of defiance, and not of fear,
A voice in the darkness, a knock at the door,
And a word that shall echo for evermore!
For, borne on the night-wind of the Past,
Through all our history, to the last,
In the hour of darkness and peril and need,
The people will waken and listen to hear
The hurrying hoof-beats of that steed,
And the midnight message of Paul Revere.

—*Henry Wadsworth Longfellow*

Name _____

Windy Nights

Whenever the moon and stars are set,
    Whenever the wind is high,
All night long in the dark and wet,
    A man goes riding by.
Late in the night when the fires are out,
    Why does he gallop and gallop about?

Whenever the trees are crying aloud,
    And the ships are tossed at sea,
By, on the highway, low and loud,
    By at the gallop goes he.
By at the gallop he goes, and then
    By he comes back at the gallop again.

—**Robert Louis Stevenson**

Name _____

O Captain! My Captain!

O Captain! my Captain! our fearful trip is done,
The ship has weather'd every rack, the prize we sought is won,
The port is near, the bells I hear, the people all exulting,
While follow eyes the steady keel, the vessel grim and daring;
    But O heart! heart! heart!
     O the bleeding drops of red,
      Where on the deck my Captain lies,
       Fallen cold and dead.

O Captain! my Captain! rise up and hear the bells;
Rise up—for you the flag is flung—for you the bugle trills,
For you bouquets and ribbon'd wreaths—for you the shores crowding,
For you they call, the swaying mass, their eager faces turning;
    Here, Captain! dear father!
     This arm beneath your head!
      It is some dream that on the deck
       You've fallen cold and dead.

My Captain does not answer, his lips are pale and still,
My father does not feel my arm, he has no pulse nor will;
The ship is anchor'd safe and sound, its voyage closed and done,
From fearful trip the victor ship comes in with object won;
    Exult, O shores! and ring, O bells!
     But I, with mournful tread,
      Walk the deck my Captain lies,
       Fallen cold and dead.

—*Walt Whitman*

Note: Walt Whitman wrote this poem following the assassination of Abraham Lincoln in 1865.

Building Fluency • EMC 3345 • © Evan-Moor Corp.

The Runaway Slave

The runaway slave came to my house and stopt outside,
I heard his motions crackling the twigs of the woodpile,
Through the swung half-door of the kitchen
    I saw him limpsy and weak,
And went where he sat on a log and led him in
    and assured him,
And brought water and fill'd a tub for his sweated
    body and bruis'd feet,
And gave him a room that enter'd from my own,
    and gave him some coarse clean clothes,
And remember perfectly well his revolving eyes
    and his awkwardness,
And remember putting plasters on the galls of his
    neck and ankles;
He staid with me a week before he was recuperated
    and pass'd north,
I had him sit next me at table, my fire-lock lean'd in the corner.

—*Walt Whitman*

Riddles, Jokes, Tongue Twisters, and Rhymes

* Transparency provided

Name _____

Out of This World

What kind of songs do planets like to sing?

(Nep-tunes!)

How did the astronaut serve dinner in outer space?

(On flying saucers!)

Where do astronauts leave their spaceships?

(At parking meteors!)

How do you get a baby astronaut to sleep?

(You rock it!)

School Riddles

What happened when Joey lost his dictionary?

(He knew he was in for a bad spell.)

What does a kid need if he is absent during final exams?

(A good excuse)

Where do books sleep?

(Under their covers)

What's white when it's dirty?

(A blackboard)

Dozen

Knock, knock.

Who's there?

Dozen!

Dozen who?

Dozen anybody want to play with me?

Ben

Knock, knock.

Who's there?

Ben.

Ben who?

Ben knocking on the door all afternoon!

Arthur

Knock, knock.

Who's there?

Arthur.

Arthur who?

Arthur more cookies in the jar?

Elephant Jokes

How do you get down from elephants?

(You don't. You get down from ducks.)

What has 6 legs, 3 ears, 4 tusks, and 2 trunks?

(An elephant with spare parts)

What's the difference between eating an elephant and eating peanut butter?

(Elephants don't stick to the roof of your mouth.)

How do you stop a charging elephant?

(Take away its credit card.)

  Building Fluency • EMC 3345 • © Evan-Moor Corp.

School Jokes

Father: How are your grades, son?

Son: Under water, Dad.

Father: Under water? What do you mean?

Son: They're below C level.

Smart student: I'm taking French, Spanish, and algebra this year.

Less smart student: Okay. Let me hear you say "good evening" in algebra.

Student: But I don't think I deserve a zero on this exam.

Teacher: Neither do I, but it's the lowest mark I can give you.

A Sad Story

A tree toad loved a she-toad

Who lived up in a tree.

He was a two-toed tree toad

But a three-toed toad was she.

The two-toed tree toad tried to win

The three-toed tree toad's heart.

For the two-toed tree toad loved the ground

That the three-toed tree toad trod.

But the two-toed tree toad tried in vain.

He couldn't please her whim.

From her tree toad bower

With her three-toed power

The she-toad vetoed him.

—Anonymous

Jolly Young Fisher

When a jolly young fisher named Fisher

Went fishing for fish in a fissure,

A fish, with a grin,

Pulled the fisherman in—

Now they're fishing the fissure for Fisher.

—Anonymous

A Good Son

"Go, my son, and shut the shutter."

This I heard a mother utter.

"Shutter's shut," the boy did mutter.

"I can't shut 'er any shutter."

They're Mine!

Quilla and Quint quarreled over the covey of quarantined quail.

Better Botter

Betty Botter had some butter,

"But," she said, "this butter's bitter.

If I bake this bitter butter,

It would make my batter bitter

But a bit of better butter—

That would make my batter better."

So she bought a bit of butter,

Better than her bitter butter,

And she baked it in her batter,

And the batter was not bitter.

So 'twas better Betty Botter

Bought a bit of better butter.

A Woodchuck

How much wood would a woodchuck chuck

if a woodchuck could chuck wood?

He would chuck, he would, as much as he could,

and chuck as much wood as a woodchuck would

if a woodchuck could chuck wood.

A Swan

Swan swam over the sea,

Swim, swan, swim!

Swan swam back again.

Well swum, swan!

Mules

On mules we find two legs behind

and two we find before.

We stand behind before we find

what those behind be for.

Name _____

Little Miss Tuckett

Little Miss Tuckett

Sat on a bucket,

Eating some peaches and cream.

There came a grasshopper

And tried hard to stop her,

But she said, "Go away, or I'll scream."

—Anonymous

Twinkle, Twinkle, Little Bat

Twinkle, twinkle, little bat!

How I wonder what you're at!

Up above the world you fly,

Like a tea tray in the sky.

—Lewis Carroll

*Note: These rhymes imitate the style of
two familiar nursery rhymes. Do you know
which ones?*

Nonfiction

* Transparency provided

Declaration of Independence

When in the Course of human events it becomes necessary for one people to dissolve the political bands which have connected them with another and to assume among the powers of the earth, the separate and equal station to which the Laws of Nature and of Nature's God entitle them, a decent respect to the opinions of mankind requires that they should declare the causes which impel them to the separation.

We hold these truths to be self-evident, that all men are created equal, that they are endowed by their Creator with certain unalienable Rights, that among these are Life, Liberty and the pursuit of Happiness. —That to secure these rights, Governments are instituted among Men, deriving their just powers from the consent of the governed,—That whenever any Form of Government becomes destructive of these ends, it is the Right of the People to alter or to abolish it, and to institute new Government, laying its foundation on such principles and organizing its powers in such form, as to them shall seem most likely to effect their Safety and Happiness.

Benjamin Franklin

Benjamin Franklin was born in 1706 in Boston, Massachusetts. He was one of seventeen children in his family! He loved books and was always full of ideas, but his family didn't have enough money to keep him in school. When he was ten, he started to work in his father's soap and candle shop. At twelve, he worked in his brother's print shop. When he was twenty-two, he set up his own print shop where he wrote and published a newspaper, *The Pennsylvania Gazette*.

Once a year, he printed *Poor Richard's Almanack*. People in that time read the *Almanack* for information on weather, recipes, important dates, stories, and wise sayings. Ben Franklin is remembered for many of those sayings, such as, "Early to bed. Early to rise. Makes a man healthy, wealthy, and wise."

In 1748, Ben retired from the publishing business. Then he spent his time helping others and inventing things. He set up Philadelphia's first fire and police departments, its first hospital, and its first lending library. He helped to write the Declaration of Independence. He traveled to France as a special ambassador. And he served as the oldest delegate to the constitutional convention.

Ben Franklin was an important man in the history of the United States.

Building Fluency • EMC 3345 • © Evan-Moor Corp.

How to Secure Houses, etc., from Lightning

It has pleased God in his goodness to mankind, at length to discover to them the means of securing their habitations and other buildings from mischief by thunder and lightning. The method is this:

Provide a small iron rod but of such a length, that one end being three or four feet in the moist ground, the other may be six or eight feet above the highest part of the building. To the upper end of the rod fasten about a foot of brass wire, the size of a common knitting-needle, sharpened to a fine point; the rod may be secured to the house by a few small staples. If the house or barn be long, there may be a rod and point at each end, and a middling wire along the ridge from one to the other.

A house thus furnished will not be damaged by lightning, it being attracted by the points, and passing thro the metal into the ground without hurting any thing. Vessels also, having a sharp pointed rod fixed on the top of their masts, with a wire from the foot of the rod reaching down, round one of the shrouds, to the water, will not be hurt by lightning.

—*From* **Poor Richard's Almanack** *by Benjamin Franklin, 1753*

The White House Burns
Washington City, August 24, 1814

British troops under the command of General Ross and Admiral Cockburn stormed the White House on August 24, 1814. Dolley Madison, the president's wife, fled from Washington City a few hours before the attack. The president was already away.

The British soldiers stuffed souvenirs inside their shirts and uniforms. They piled paintings, draperies, and furnishings in the center of each of the rooms. Even the pianoforte was pushed into the pile.

After the soldiers left the White House, flaming torches, pine poles topped with cotton, were rushed into the president's house. The furniture was set on fire. As the White House went up in flames, the gunpowder stored in the basement exploded. The White House was destroyed along with many other buildings in our nation's capital.

Today, Washington City is a mass of rubble, ashes, and debris. The priceless Congressional Library has been destroyed. Only the U.S. patent office was saved.

Building Fluency • EMC 3345 • © Evan-Moor Corp.

Name _____

The Gettysburg Address
Abraham Lincoln

Fourscore and seven years ago our fathers brought forth on this continent, a new nation, conceived in Liberty, and dedicated to the proposition that all men are created equal.

Now we are engaged in a great civil war, testing whether that nation, or any nation so conceived and so dedicated, can long endure. We are met on a great battlefield of that war. We have come to dedicate a portion of that field, as a final resting place for those who here gave their lives that this nation might live. It is altogether fitting and proper that we should do this.

But, in a larger sense, we cannot dedicate—we cannot consecrate—we cannot hallow—this ground. The brave men, living and dead, who struggled here, have consecrated it, far above our poor power to add or detract. The world will little note, nor long remember what we say here, but it can never forget what they did here. It is for us the living, rather, to be dedicated here to the unfinished work which they who fought here have thus far so nobly advanced. It is rather for us to be here dedicated to the great task remaining before us—that from these honored dead we take increased devotion to that cause for which they gave the last full measure of devotion—that we here highly resolve that these dead shall not have died in vain—that this nation, under God, shall have a new birth of freedom—and that government of the people, by the people, for the people, shall not perish from the earth.

Name _____

Totem Poles—Faces of Wood

Have you ever seen a totem pole? These tall wooden structures are very common in the northwestern part of the United States and Canada. Native Americans carved totem poles. The animals and other figures on the poles told stories about a family's history or stories from its culture.

Cedar is the best kind of wood to use for a totem pole. First, the tree is cut down. The bark is then cut off, and the tree is hollowed and shaped. Finally, the features are carved into the pole. Some poles are painted with bright colors.

Early Native Americans used sharpened shells, stones, or bones to carve their poles. Later, they used iron knives and other tools. Today, some carvers even use chain saws!

In the past, some totem poles were placed on the beach to welcome visitors to a village. Others were placed in front of the house. Sometimes, a totem pole was part of the house itself!

Native American society has changed a lot in the past 200 years. The art of carving totem poles was almost lost. Fortunately, museums and Native American societies have tried to keep the art of totem poles alive. Today, young carvers can still learn the art of creating a story out of wood.

Name _____

Terry Fox

In 1977 at the age of 19, Terry Fox was diagnosed with bone cancer. A tumor in his right leg caused the bone to become soft. Doctors amputated the leg about six inches above the knee and fitted him with a prosthetic leg. Just three weeks after the surgery, Terry was walking on his new leg. Soon after, he was running.

Terry decided to run a marathon. Running was very difficult because the stump of his leg would bleed. Doctors built a new leg for Terry using a motorcycle shock absorber to ease the stress on his stump. The new leg helped, but running was still painful. In spite of the pain, Terry finished his marathon.

That achievement gave Terry an unusual idea. He planned to run all the way across Canada to raise money for cancer research. On April 12, 1980, Terry began his heroic run, which he called the Marathon of Hope. At St. John's, Newfoundland, he dipped his foot into the chilly waters of the Atlantic Ocean and began to run.

Every day, Terry ran 26 miles. As the weeks and months went by, people began to pay attention to Terry's run. Television cameras followed him. People lined the streets to watch Terry run, and donations began to pour in.

But Terry began to get sick. Near the city of Thunder Bay, Ontario, he could go no farther. The cancer had spread to his lungs. Terry battled the disease for ten more months and finally died on June 28, 1981, just one month before his 23rd birthday.

Today, Terry Fox Runs are held in over 60 countries. More than $350 million has been raised in his memory. Terry Fox was unable to finish his race, but his hope and vision continue to inspire others.

Bighorn Sheep

Every autumn, high in the Rocky Mountains of the American West, a dramatic battle takes place. Bighorn rams—the males of the species—challenge each other to combat as part of their mating ritual. The rams, whose large curled horns can weigh up to 30 pounds, charge toward each other. They race at speeds up to 20 miles per hour, slamming their heads together with tremendous force. The clash of their massive horns rings through the mountains like the sound of gigantic hammer blows.

A bighorn ram may weigh up to 350 pounds, but can move easily along steep slopes and rocky ledges. Although bighorns are brawny and muscular, they are agile. They skip nimbly along narrow mountain trails only an inch or two in width. Now and then, a bighorn sheep will lose its footing and tumble to its death. But the steep mountainsides help to protect the bighorns from predators such as wolves, mountain lions, and coyotes.

Hunting, disease, and habitat destruction over the years have brought the bighorn sheep to the brink of extinction. Today, hunting of bighorn sheep is carefully controlled. Populations are slowly recovering, but remain small with many groups numbering fewer than 100 animals.

The Rocky Mountain bighorn sheep has long been a majestic symbol of the American West. Today, volunteer organizations work hard to protect the habitats of these amazing animals. They want to make sure that bighorn sheep will endure the next 200 years, dancing along the high ridges and thrilling new generations of wildlife watchers.

Name _____

An Extreme Continent

The continent of Antarctica is a land of extremes. It is located farther south than any of the other six continents and includes the geographic South Pole. Ninety-eight percent of Antarctica is covered with ice.

The coldest temperature ever recorded on Earth— −128.6° Fahrenheit—was measured on Antarctica. Due to the cold, very little moisture evaporates. Over time, the snow has built up into a massive sheet of ice that covers most of the continent. The rest of the continent, about 2%, is rock.

Scientists believe that 500 million years ago Antarctica was located near Earth's equator. The continent's climate was also very different. Dinosaur fossils found in Antarctica show how dramatically the continent has changed.

Today, however, there are no trees or bushes on Antarctica. Plant life is limited to mosses, lichens, and algae. Most of the region's larger animals, such as penguins and seals, spend most of their time in the waters around the frozen continent. Mites, ticks, and worms are among Antarctica's most common land animals. There are no permanent human residents on the continent, although scientists spend time at research bases.

Antarctic Expedition

Ernest Shackleton wanted to be the first explorer to reach the South Pole. It was Roald Amundsen, however, who claimed that honor in 1911. Disappointed, Shackleton announced he would be the first explorer to cross the entire Antarctic continent—on foot!

In August 1914, Shackleton's ship *Endurance* set sail from England. After a stopover on South Georgia Island, the *Endurance* headed south and in January entered the pack ice of the Weddell Sea. The ship became completely trapped in an ice floe. Huge blocks of ice crushed the sides of the ship, and it sprung leaks. Shackleton ordered the crew to abandon ship. On November 21, 1915, the crew watched the *Endurance* sink. With three lifeboats and limited supplies, they were trapped hundreds of miles from land.

Over the next five months, Shackleton's crew lived on an ice floe. Supplies ran out, and blizzards raged on. In April, the ice began to break apart. The lifeboats were launched. Shackleton knew the crew could not make it 700 miles (1,122 km) to South Georgia Island. So they traveled to nearby Elephant Island instead.

Elephant Island was a deserted wasteland. The crew ate seals and sucked on ice to survive. Knowing his crew would not last long, Shackleton made a difficult decision. He and five of his crew would travel to South Georgia Island to get help. He would leave twenty-two men behind.

After seventeen treacherous days at sea, Shackleton's crew reached the island where they found help. Fishermen helped get a boat for Shackleton. But because of rough seas, it took three months, and four attempts, to save all his crew on Elephant Island.

In 1919, Shackleton wrote about this amazing survival story in a book entitled *South*.

Building Fluency • EMC 3345 • © Evan-Moor Corp.

Father of Our National Parks

John Muir moved to America when he was eleven years old. Muir grew up working long hours on a farm. Whenever he could get away, he wandered into the countryside. That's where his curiosity with the natural world started.

On one of Muir's first nature trips, he walked 1,000 miles (1,600 km) from Indiana to the Gulf of Mexico. Muir kept a journal of all he saw in nature. Then he sailed to Cuba. Later, he went to Panama. From Panama, Muir sailed up the West Coast to San Francisco. From then on, California was Muir's home.

In San Francisco, Muir asked the first person he saw where the most beautiful place in California was. That person pointed east and said, "The Sierra Nevada." Muir walked there and fell in love with the scenery. He saw how the sunlight seemed to light up the mountains with their beauty. Muir later wrote of the Sierras, "They should be called the 'Range of Light'—they are the most beautiful of all the mountain chains I have ever seen."

In the heart of the Sierras is Yosemite. Muir noticed that sheep and cattle were destroying the meadows of Yosemite. He called the animals "hoofed locusts." He brought attention to Yosemite and helped make it a national park in 1890. Later, Muir helped create other national parks. He became friends with President Theodore Roosevelt. In 1903, Roosevelt visited Muir in Yosemite. Together, they talked about preserving many of America's natural treasures. Because of that, Muir is called the "Father of Our National Parks."

Muir's efforts to preserve nature helped start a group called the Sierra Club. The Sierra Club has worked for over one hundred years to preserve special places in nature from being destroyed. Muir was the club's first president. He said he helped start the club to "make the mountains glad."

"Pap" Singleton: A Man with a Dream

After the Civil War, African Americans in the South were freed from slavery, but they were still terribly poor. One of these former slaves was a man named Benjamin Singleton. He wanted to help himself and others with similar problems.

Singleton heard about opportunities in Kansas. There was plenty of land available. Settlers were encouraged to come help develop this rich land. He believed that former slaves could make better lives for themselves if they only had the chance to own land.

It was not hard for Singleton to persuade people from the South to follow him to Kansas. Although black people in the South were free, they still were not treated well. They were forced to live as second-class citizens. More than 50,000 African Americans left the South in the late 1870s.

"Pap" Singleton, as he was known, founded two different settlements in Kansas. Many who followed him to Kansas became successful farmers. Their dreams came true.

How to Build a Sand Castle

Building a sand castle can be tricky. If you dig a hole too close to the shoreline, the castle may get washed out by waves. If you are too far from the shore, you will have to dig a very deep hole in order to reach wet sand. However, for an almost perfect sand castle, just follow the guidelines below.

After choosing a good spot, dig a hole and place the scooped-out sand next to it. Fill a bucket with seawater and keep it next to your hole. You are now ready to start building your sand castle.

Start by using moist sand to make a flat, even base for your castle. Next, use more of this sand to build layers. Think of how a grand, layered wedding cake is stacked with each layer getting smaller as it reaches the top. The easiest way to do this is to sprinkle handfuls of sand onto the base and then gently flatten them and mold them into a circular shape. Each layer should have a smaller circumference than the previous one. Use wet sand to even out and smooth the tower layers.

Finally, you are ready to build the walls. Use your bucket of seawater to wet some sand. Grab a handful of sand and flatten it between your palms. Use your hands to shape it into a brick or block. Next, place the sand brick about six inches away from the tower. Make more sand bricks and place them side by side, creating a circle around the tower. Now, stand back and admire your sand castle.

Name _____

Bike Helmets Are Cool!

There are 28 million children, ages 5 to 14, who ride bicycles in this country. Riding bicycles is fun and good exercise when you ride safely. Unfortunately, thousands of children are disabled or die each year as a result of bike accidents. Experts say wearing one piece of equipment—a helmet—can help save children.

Today's bike helmets are lightweight and comfortable. A safe helmet has a Consumer Product Safety Commission sticker inside. This means it has been tested for safety. But if a helmet has been in a crash, it should be replaced. Damaged helmets lose their ability to absorb shock.

Wearing bike helmets saves lives. But estimates show that only about 15 to 25 percent of children who ride bikes wear a helmet. Children give excuses for not wearing a helmet. Some say it's uncomfortable. Problems occur when children wear helmets that are too small or too big. Children should not borrow other people's helmets. The helmets need to fit just right.

Some children think it isn't cool to wear bike helmets. But you definitely won't look cool if you crash and do damage to your body. Studies show that 90 percent of deaths due to head injuries could be prevented by wearing helmets. Adding fluorescent, reflective stickers to helmets will make them look cooler.

You probably think little kids get into more accidents. The truth is that boys between the ages of 10 and 14 are more likely to be injured or even killed in bike accidents.

Some people think they don't need to wear helmets because they're riding close to home. Studies show that most bike crashes occur within one mile of home. About 75 percent of child bike-accident deaths occur where driveways, alleys, and streets intersect.

Now you know the facts. And yes, it *is* cool to ride your bike safely!

Building Fluency • EMC 3345 • © Evan-Moor Corp.

Fiction

* Transparency provided

The Day Pecos Bill Rode Old Twister

You've probably heard about Pecos Bill, the Texas wrangler who was as tall as a two-story house and as strong as an ox. When it was time to round up the cattle and drive them to Abilene, Bill just pointed his nose toward the sky and let out a coyote howl that echoed across Texas. The cattle thought there were a hundred or so coyotes coming after them. They were so spooked, they stampeded in the other direction as fast as they could. Pecos Bill had cowpunchers stationed all along the trail. They kept the cattle running in the right direction. When the cattle slowed down, Bill just let loose with another howl. The cattle kept running until they all reached Abilene in record time.

You might think it was strange that Bill could howl like that. Bill, you see, came by it naturally because coyotes raised him. Some folks say he thought he was a coyote until he was fourteen years old. Seems he got lost from his folks when they were moving west. But that's a story for another day.

Bein' pretty much like a coyote, Bill would stop to sniff about every now and then. He could smell almost anything in the air a hundred miles away. One morning, he said, "Better head for the cellars. There's a twister coming!" Bill put his ear to the ground. "It just passed by El Paso, and it's an hour away."

That was enough time to get some of the cattle into the tunnel Bill had dug out using Rattler, his pet snake, as a drill. As soon as everything was in order, the cowhands headed for the cellars.

"You coming in?" yelled Cowpoke Carl.

"I'm gonna ride this one out!" shouted Bill.

Carl shut the wood cover to the cellar and bolted it in place.

As for the rest of the story, this here's how Bill told it when he showed up a week or two later. There isn't any doubt it was the truth. Bill was as truthful as a Sunday school teacher.

It seems Bill and his horse, Widow Maker, waited until Old Twister came roaring across the ranch like an angry panther chasing its dinner. When it caught sight of Bill, it took out after him.

Bill led Old Twister away from the barns and the bunkhouse as far as he could. Widow Maker managed to dance to the side each time Twister came close to Bill. That big wind was racing at such a speed, it could only twirl straight ahead like a ballerina spinning across the stage. It couldn't keep up with Widow Maker's fancy stepping. Old Twister was getting uglier by the minute. It wasn't used to playing a losing game of tag. It was clear to Bill that Old Twister wouldn't slow down until it tore up the whole ranch, and him, too.

"I've tamed bears, snakes, and wolves," Bill said to Widow Maker. "I guess it's time I took the fight out of a twister. My rope's ready, and I'm going for the ride of my life. Widow Maker, you head out as far away from me and this bag-of-wind as you can. Leave the rest to me." Bill sent his rope whirling into the air faster than a bolt of lightning. It dropped over the top of Old Twister and headed for the middle of that windy monster. Bill tightened the rope and gripped the end. Hanging on like a flea on a dog, he jumped onto the side of the twister and climbed toward the top. Old Twister danced, hopped, and nearly turned itself wrong side out trying to shake Bill off. It was some fight, but Bill never did give up. He just climbed higher, poking his spurs right into Old Twister's sides.

When Bill reached the top, he was a little worse for wear. His hair stood straight up like the points on a picket fence, and his leather shirt was so fringed it looked like blades of brown prairie grass. Nonetheless, he was as calm as a hibernating bear. He rode bareback on the rim of that twister, and looked down inside.

There was a city's worth of houses, a herd or two of cattle, and everything else you could need just swirling around inside. Old Twister bucked and kicked up its tail like a bucking bronco at a rodeo. It didn't do any good. Bill rode Old Twister like he was a kid riding on a rocking horse.

Now Bill was having so much fun, he decided there ought to be some good done along the way. It was a shame to let Old Twister smash up all those houses. People moving west had a long stretch to travel without a town. Bill reached down inside, and one by one he tossed the houses behind Old Twister. The houses settled down in neat rows, making up the prettiest town you could imagine. Now, when people crossed that long, dry stretch of prairie, they'd have a place to stop and rest.

Bill scooped up all the grass and plants inside the twister and threw them into a giant stack near the town. He dug in his spurs each time the twister tried to roar off across the prairie. While the twister spun around in circles going nowhere, Bill was scooping out the cattle and dropping them onto the stack of grass. They'd have enough to eat until the next wagon train came rumbling along. When Bill finished, it looked like a fine place to settle down. One day, Bill planned to do just that.

Old Twister was empty now and as tired as a mother hen that had spent the day chasing after her chicks. Bill led Old Twister back the way it came. By the time Bill was back at the ranch, Old Twister was a little breeze as gentle as a newborn lamb frolicking across a meadow. Bill had had enough traveling for a while. He went back to howling at the moon and riding Widow Maker around the ranch.

www.TripToCollege.org

How the Big Dipper Came to Be

Long, long ago, there were five wolves. They were all brothers who traveled together. They hunted meat for food, and they always shared it with Coyote.

One evening, Coyote noticed that the wolves were all looking up at the sky. "What are you looking at up there?" asked Coyote.

"There are two animals up there," replied the oldest wolf. "But we can't get to them."

"That is easy," said Coyote. He took his bow and shot an arrow into the sky where it stuck. Then he shot another, which stuck into the first. Then, he shot another and another until the chain of arrows reached the ground.

The oldest wolf took the first step. His dog followed him. Then the other four wolf brothers trotted up the ladder, and Coyote brought up the rear. They climbed and climbed. They traveled for many days and nights. Their paws were bleeding and their legs were shaking. Finally, they reached the sky.

The wolves, the dog, and Coyote stood in the sky and stared at the two animals that the wolves had seen from below. The animals were two grizzly bears.

Coyote was afraid. "Don't go near them," he warned. "Those grizzlies will tear you apart." But the two youngest wolves had already headed over toward the bears. The next two wolves followed closely behind. Only the oldest wolf and his dog stayed back. The four wolves plopped down and stared at the bears. When the oldest wolf saw that it was safe, he trotted over with his dog and joined his brothers.

Coyote refused to come over. He did not trust the bears. But Coyote was thinking. He thought to himself, "That sure makes a nice picture. They all look good sitting there like that. I think I'll leave it that way for everyone to see. Then when people gaze up at the sky, they will say, 'That picture is so beautiful there must be a story about it. I wonder who placed those stars to create such a beautiful scene,' and they will tell a story about me."

Coyote left the wolves, the dog, and the bears sitting that way. As he climbed back down to Earth, he pulled the arrows out of the sky one by one so there was no way for anyone to get up or down. When he reached Earth, Coyote gazed up and admired the picture he had left up in the sky.

The picture has been there ever since. Today, people call it the Big Dipper. If you look closely enough, you will see that three wolves make up the handle, and the oldest one still has his dog with him. The two youngest wolves make up the part of the bowl under the handle, and the two grizzly bears make up the other side that points to the North Star.

How the Finch Got Her Colors

Long, long ago, all the birds were gray. Their feathers had no colors at all. One day, the Great Bird who ruled them all gazed at a rainbow in the sky. The rainbow gave the Great Bird a brilliant idea. He called all the birds together and told them to line up before him.

"I am going to give each one of you some of these wonderful colors," announced the Great Bird.

The birds were so excited that they began to squawk and to push and shove each other with their wings. They all wanted to be at the head of the line. The noise was deafening.

"I want blue!" shrieked the jay.

"Give me yellow!" warbled the oriole.

The parrot squawked, "I get orange and green!"

"Out of the way!" whistled the cardinal. "Red is my color!"

The greedy birds beat each other with their wings and pecked each other with their beaks as they fought over the colors.

Finally, all the colors of the rainbow had been taken, and the birds lined up in front of the Great Bird to show him their wonderful new feathers. Then the Great Bird spied the finch. She was still as gray and plain as always.

"Finch, why didn't you choose a color?" asked the Great Bird gently.

"Well, I wanted a color," peeped the finch sadly, "and I was waiting for my turn. Everybody cut in ahead of me, and now all the colors are gone." Finch brushed a pale wing across her black eyes.

The Great Bird put his wings on his hips and glared angrily at all the other birds. "You selfish, greedy things!" he screeched. "I have a good mind to take all your colors away so that you will all be gray again!"

The birds looked around at one another, feeling slightly ashamed.

"But," the Great Bird continued, "I'll take just a little bit of each color from you and give them to the finch. Pass before me, please, and no ducking out of line!"

So the birds walked slowly past the Great Bird. Not a sound could be heard. Great Bird took a bit of blue, a dab of yellow, some green, a pinch of red, a smear of pink—some of every color—and gave them all to the finch. Then he blended the colors on her feathers, shading them just right, and smoothed them with the tip of his wing.

Finch spread her wings and admired the rich mix of colors gleaming in the sun. "Thank you, Great Bird," she tweeted.

And that is the way the finch is to this very day.

Building Fluency • EMC 3345 • © Evan-Moor Corp.

How Butterflies Came to Be

Long, long ago, when the Earth was very new, Elder Brother walked around to enjoy the beauty. He gazed at the children playing. Everywhere on Earth, they were playing joyfully.

Elder Brother appreciated the children's happiness. He saw how they loved the soft green grass, the colors of flowers, the sweet songs of birds, and the soft rain. He saw how the children loved the bright leaves that fall from the trees and fly around in the breeze.

As he watched, Elder Brother started to worry. He thought, "This joy may fly away some day, and these children will be sad. They might get sick or be hungry. They might get cold in the snow, or be blown about by harsh winds."

Then Elder Brother had a brainstorm that made him happy again. He picked up a big deerskin bag and filled it with flowers and red and yellow leaves. He added some blue feathers of the jaybird, some blades of green grass, and some golden corn kernels. He dropped in a handful of sunshine. At the very last minute, he threw in some bird songs. Then Elder Brother grasped the top of the bag in his large hands and shook it many times so that everything was mixed together.

When he had mixed everything, Elder Brother called to the children, "Now come here and open this bag!"

When the bag was opened, out fluttered thousands of shiny, airy, colorful creatures with wings. They were the colors of all things on Earth, and each creature sang a different song.

The children laughed and clapped with joy as they chased the wonderful creatures. "What are they? What are they?" the children shouted.

"These are my gift to you," said Elder Brother. "They are called butterflies. If sad times come, the sight of butterflies may cheer you up. On cold, stormy days when the rain beats down, the memory of butterflies will warm your heart."

But the birds were not as happy as the children were.

"Elder Brother," the birds squawked, "at the very beginning of the world, colors were given to all living things. Songs were given only to us birds. We don't think it's fair that these new creatures should have our songs!"

Elder Brother thought it over. Then he replied, "Birds, you are right. Your songs are special, and they should belong only to you."

And that is how it is to this very day. The butterflies dance and fly and make the children happy. But they are silent. Only the birds can sing.

The Earth and Sky

Sagbata and Sogbo, the sons of the goddess Mawu, shared the task of ruling the world and the heavens. Unfortunately, the two brothers could not agree on anything, not even the color of the clouds.

Mawu would not take one side of the argument or the other. "You have to learn to get along," she said.

Sagbata, the older brother, packed up all their treasures. "I can't remain in the sky with you any longer. You won't listen to anything I say. Since I am the older brother, all treasures belong to me. I'm taking them to Earth. I leave water and fire here with you because I have no way to carry them."

"The sooner you go, the better," Sogbo said.

After Sagbata left, Sogbo became the favorite of his mother and the other deities. They allowed him to do whatever pleased him. To get even with his brother, who was caring for the Earth, Sogbo kept the rain in the sky and would not allow any water to fall on the Earth.

The plants didn't grow, and the people and animals were hungry. The people went to Sagbata and complained. "Why should we worship you when the Earth burns and there is no water? Go back to the sky. We lived well before you descended to Earth. You bring us misfortune."

"The rains will come," Sagbata said. Weeks, months, and years passed. It didn't rain.

Sagbata called two sky prophets to him and asked them why it didn't rain. "Your brother is holding back the rain. Until you can live peacefully, the rain will stay in the sky," they told him.

"I can't climb back to the sky to talk to my brother. It's too far. What can I do?"

"Call the wututu bird and ask him to take a message to your brother. If you offer to share the Earth, he might share the rain," the sky prophets said.

The wututu bird answered Sagbata's call. "Take this message to my brother," requested Sagbata. "Tell him that I have been selfish. I will let him rule the Earth with me. He can care for the villages and all the people."

The wututu bird flew back to the land of the sky and delivered the message to Sogbo. "Tell Sagbata that I will agree to help him rule the Earth," replied Sogbo.

The wututu bird flew back to Earth. Before he had returned to Sagbata, it began to rain. Sagbata greeted the bird and said, "I know my brother has accepted my offer. Because you have served the two of us well, I will tell all people on Earth that you are sacred and cannot be harmed."

The two brothers became good friends. The wututu bird carried messages of goodwill from one brother to the other. The grass and plants grew again, and the people weren't hungry any more.

Building Fluency • EMC 3345 • © Evan-Moor Corp.

Readers' Theater

* Transparency provided

Readers' Theater

WHAT IS READERS' THEATER?

Readers' Theater is a minimalist way to perform plays. No costumes, props, or scenery are required. Students stand in front of an audience, scripts held in their hands or set on music stands. Very little movement is necessary. Readers' Theater provides the value of performing plays without the logistical considerations.

WHY PERFORM READERS' THEATER?

Readers' Theater yields positive growth in reading skills. Classroom research indicates that students strengthen word recognition, fluency, and comprehension by practicing and performing Readers' Theater selections. In addition, students love to perform, and this enthusiasm carries over to many other aspects of the school day.

HOW DO I START?

Monday

- The teacher introduces or reviews the basics of Readers' Theater.

- Using the transparency copy on the overhead, the teacher reads the play through once, modeling how to read each part.

- The teacher assigns parts, or students volunteer for parts. At first, the teacher should assign parts. As the students gain experience with Readers' Theater procedures and become more fluent readers, they can volunteer or assign parts themselves.

Tuesday through Thursday

- The teacher creates various practice opportunities—individual, group, and home sessions.

Friday

- Select the performance time. Make it a special event, such as a festival on a Friday afternoon.

- Invite an audience. Classmates, another class, parents, or the principal and office staff make good audiences.

- Consider performing for an off-site audience within walking distance.

 Building Fluency • EMC 3345 • © Evan-Moor Corp.

Name _____

The Greedy Little Cat

Characters

Greedy Cat	**Parrot**
Old Woman	**Man**
Teacher	**Students**
Street Musicians	**Tailor**
Narrator 1	**Narrator 2**

Narrator 1: One afternoon, Parrot invited his friend Greedy Cat over for lunch. Parrot made a great platter of butter cakes, a huge bowl of ripe fruit, and a sizzling skillet of spicy chops.

Narrator 2: Greedy Cat knocked at the door promptly at noon. He and Parrot sat down to eat the delicious meal.

Greedy Cat: Thank you for inviting me to lunch, friend Parrot. I am very hungry indeed.

Narrator 1: And Greedy Cat began to eat. He ate the pile of butter cakes, and then he ate the platter. He slurped down all the ripe fruit, and then he swallowed the bowl. He gobbled up the spicy chops and the sizzling skillet, too.

Narrator 2: Parrot watched in astonishment and tried to control his growing irritation.

Greedy Cat: That was a fine meal, but I am still hungry. Have you anything else to eat?

Parrot: Why, no, Greedy Cat. You have eaten every morsel. I did not get so much as a mouthful. I have nothing else to offer you. Unless of course, you wish to eat me!

Greedy Cat: Hmmm. That is not a bad idea!

Narrator 1: And Greedy Cat swallowed Parrot in one gulp.

Narrator 2: An old woman passing by the window saw this evil deed.

Old Woman: Shame on you, Greedy Cat! What have you done?

Greedy Cat: I ate the cakes and the platter, the fruit and the bowl, the spicy chops and the sizzling skillet, and my friend Parrot. And I am still hungry, so I shall swallow you, too!

Narrator 1: And so he did. Then Greedy Cat strolled out of the house to stretch his legs and get some fresh air. He saw a man riding a donkey up the lane.

Man: Get out of the way, Greedy Cat. I don't want my donkey to tread on you.

Greedy Cat: Ha! I'm not worried about a silly old donkey! I ate the cakes and the platter, the fruit and the bowl, the spicy chops and the sizzling skillet, my friend Parrot, and an old woman. And I am still hungry, so I shall swallow you and your donkey, too!

Narrator 2: And so he did. Then he continued down the lane where some students from a nearby school were taking a walk with their teacher.

Teacher and Students: Good afternoon, Greedy Cat! How are you?

Greedy Cat: I'm delightfully well, thank you very much. I ate the cakes and the platter, the fruit and the bowl, the spicy chops and the sizzling skillet, my friend Parrot, the old woman, and the man with a donkey. And I am still hungry, so I shall swallow you, too!

Narrator 1: And so he did. Then he waddled along the lane until he came to a band of street musicians who were playing a merry tune on their instruments.

Street Musicians: Greetings, Greedy Cat! Isn't it a fine day?

Greedy Cat: It's quite lovely. In fact, it would be a perfect day if I were not so very hungry.

Street Musicians: Haven't you had your lunch, Greedy Cat?

Greedy Cat: Oh yes. I ate the cakes and the platter, the fruit and the bowl, the spicy chops and the sizzling skillet, my friend Parrot, the old woman, the man with a donkey, and the teacher with her students. But I am still hungry, so I shall swallow you, too!

Narrator 2: And so he did. Then the Greedy Cat sat down on a park bench to rest for a little while. Along came the town tailor.

Tailor: Hello, Greedy Cat. I see you are enjoying the sunshine.

Greedy Cat: Yes, it is pleasant enough. But it would be more pleasant if I had a snack to eat.

Tailor: You're in luck, Greedy Cat. I have a cookie here in my work basket that I will gladly give you.

Greedy Cat: Why thank you! I ate the cakes and the platter, the fruit and the bowl, the spicy chops and the sizzling skillet, the old woman, the man with a donkey, the teacher with her students, and the street musicians. But I am still hungry, so I shall swallow you and your cookie, too!

Narrator 1: And so he did. But as soon as the little tailor slid down the Greedy Cat's gullet, he drew his sharp scissors from his work basket. With two snips and a snap, he cut a neat opening in Greedy Cat's belly and popped out into the fresh air.

Narrator 2: Parrot, the old woman, the man and his donkey, the teacher and her students, and the street musicians with their instruments scrambled out close behind him. They thanked the tailor profusely and hurried away to their respective homes.

Narrator 1: But the kindly tailor took a sharp needle and some strong silk thread and sewed the little cat up again, good as new.

Narrator 2: And Greedy Cat went home and bandaged his sore tummy and didn't even think about eating again for a whole, entire week.

    Building Fluency • EMC 3345 • © Evan-Moor Corp.

Name _____

Toads and Diamonds

Narrator 1: Once upon a time, there lived a woman and her two daughters. The elder daughter, Regina, and her mother were much alike. Both were disagreeable and proud and had never a kind word to say to anybody.

Narrator 2: The younger daughter, Bethany, on the other hand, had a sweet temper and a kind heart, which showed in her lovely face.

Narrator 3: The mother was partial to Regina, of course, because they were kindred spirits. She was nasty to Bethany and made her do all the scullery work.

Mother: Bethany, take this pitcher and go down to the spring. And hurry up about it! Your sister wants a cool drink. Now go!

Bethany: Yes, mother. I will gladly fetch the water.

Narrator 1: Now, the spring was two miles away, and the day was unpleasantly warm. But Bethany picked up the pitcher and set out.

Narrator 2: She was just filling her pitcher at the spring when a ragged old woman shuffled out of the woods.

Old Woman: Girl, I am weary and thirsty. Do let me have a drink of cool water.

Bethany: Of course. Let me help you.

Narrator 3: And Bethany held the cool pitcher to the old woman's lips while she drank her fill.

Old Woman: I thank you for your kindness and good manners. I give you a gift: For every word you speak, a diamond or ruby shall fall from your lips.

Narrator 1: The old woman, who was really a fairy in disguise, limped back into the woods, humming a tune and leaving Bethany to refill her pitcher and hurry home.

Mother: Where have you been, you lazy girl? Can't you see that your sister is fainting for lack of water?

Bethany: I beg your pardon, Mother.

Narrator 2: At these words, two bright diamonds and three perfect rubies fell from Bethany's lips and dropped to the floor.

Mother: What sort of trick is this?

Bethany: It is no trick, Mother. It happened at the spring.

Narrator 3: And Bethany told her mother what had transpired, while rubies and diamonds gathered in heaps about her feet.

Mother: Regina, come here this minute! Your sister is breathing riches. You, too, must have this gift. Run quickly now. Go to the spring. If an old woman asks for a drink, give it to her. And mind your manners. Oh, the riches you shall have, my love. Hurry!

Regina: Are you serious, Mother? Surely you don't expect me to walk all the way to the spring in this heat! I shall ruin my slippers!

Mother: Stop your grousing! I'll ruin more than your slippers if you don't go! Now, get!

Narrator 1: Regina took her mother's finest filigreed pitcher from the cupboard and flounced out of the house.

Narrator 2: As soon as Regina arrived at the spring, she saw a princess in a gossamer gown emerge from the woods. Of course, this was actually the same fairy, appearing in a different form.

Princess: Good day, young lady. Would you kindly draw me a pitcher of water?

Regina: Do you think I am a serving girl? Get your own drink!

Princess: My, but you are disagreeable. But though you will not oblige me with a drink, still I will give you a gift.

Narrator 3: At the mention of gifts, Regina's eyes lit up and her contemptuous expression changed to an expectant smile.

Princess: This is your gift: For every word you speak, a toad or snake shall fall from your lips.

Narrator 1: And the princess walked calmly away, leaving Regina in abject tears. When Regina at last gathered herself and returned home, her mother met her at the door.

Mother: Why do you look so downcast, my darling?

Regina: Oh, Mother! What a disaster!

Narrator 2: As Regina spoke, three lumpy toads and two green snakes slithered from her lips while her mother looked on in horror.

Narrator 3: As the years passed, Regina learned that it was best for her to remain silent, and so the house was more peaceful than it had ever been before.

Narrator 1: But Bethany, because of her good and generous nature, sang all the day and thus provided her mother and sister with all that they needed and much that they wanted.

Narrator 2: And the moral of the story?

Narrator 3: Well, that's for you to decide.

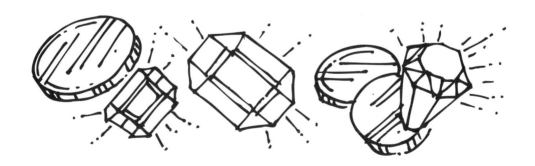

 Building Fluency • EMC 3345 • © Evan-Moor Corp.

The Adventures of Buzz and Betty

Characters

Buzz	**Betty**
Mr. Green	**Narrator**
Radio Announcer	**Singers**

Announcer: Welcome, boys and girls! Today's episode of *Buzz and Betty* is entitled "The Mystery at Big Lake." But now, kids, it's time to hear from our sponsor, No Holes Toothpaste!

Singers: If you want no holes in your teeth
Brush on top and underneath.
Use No Holes Toothpaste. It'll work for you!
No Holes Toothpaste. It tastes good, too!

Announcer: That's right, folks. Mom and Pop and kids of all ages. No Holes Toothpaste helps fight cavities. Bring some home today! And tomorrow, as every Friday on *The Adventures of Buzz and Betty,* No Holes Toothpaste will have a clue for you. The clue will help you solve this week's mystery. Remember, to solve the clue you need to have the Buzz and Betty decoder ring. You can get it by sending in two box tops of No Holes Toothpaste.

As we begin today's story, Buzz and Betty are getting ready to join their friends at a picnic. It started out as just another ordinary day for them, when suddenly…

Betty: Hello?

Mr. Green: *(in a panic)* Hello, Betty? I need you and Buzz to come down to the bank right away. I've just been robbed. The robber has gotten away! I need your help.

Betty: Gee, Mr. Green. We were going to Big Lake for a picnic. Sounds like that will have to wait. We'll come down to the bank right away!

Mr. Green: Thanks, Betty. Please hurry!

Narrator: Quick as bunnies, Betty and Buzz hurried out of the house. This was the second time the bad guys hit the bank. The two young detectives knew the crooks had to be caught before they robbed again.

Buzz: I'll come with you, Betty. I'm turning myself into a fly right now. I'll buzz around the area. Maybe I can spot the robbers. Let's go!

Narrator: Betty raced to the bank, arriving out of breath.

Betty: I came as fast as I could, Mr. Green.

Mr. Green: Good to see you, Betty. Where is your brother, Buzz?

Betty: Oh, he'll be here shortly.

Mr. Green: Why does he always show up at the end? And why do you do all the detective work? Hey, what is that buzzing around your head?

Betty: Oh, never mind that, Mr. Green. It's just a fly. Anyway, I think that…

Mr. Green: Here, let me get that darn fly…

Betty: No! Mr. Green, really! Leave it alone!

Mr. Green: It's okay. I have a big flyswatter right here.

Betty: No!

Announcer: So, tune in next time, boys and girls, for another exciting episode of *The Adventures of Buzz and Betty!* Until tomorrow, this is your announcer for No Holes Toothpaste, saying, "Stay alert!"

Name _____

Tawb the Snake and Abner the Crow

················· *Characters* ·················

Narrator 1   Narrator 2

Tawb   Mouse

Abner

Narrator 1: One sunny day, Abner the crow was sitting on his usual perch on the highest branch of an ancient oak tree overlooking the forest floor. As he gazed idly about, he noticed an unusual sight. Tawb, the old snake who lived in a den at the foot of Abner's tree, had left his hole. He was slithering quietly along the forest floor.

Narrator 2: Now, this was unusual because Tawb almost never left the comfort of his hole. In fact, he was known far and wide for his extreme laziness. Indeed, Abner could see that Tawb was flabby and out of shape from the sedentary life he led down in his burrow. While old Tawb moved slowly along the ground, Abner observed a small gray mouse heading toward the tricky old serpent.

Narrator 1: The snake saw the little rodent, too. He stopped moving and lay very still in the grass. As the mouse made his way along the forest trail, unaware of what was waiting for him, Tawb slithered into view.

Tawb: Hello, little mouse. I have a proposition for you.

Mouse: What is it, Mr. Snake?

Tawb: I am hungry, little mouse, and if you don't bring me the egg of a bird, I am going to eat you!

Narrator 1: Tawb attempted a smile, but the effort only made his features more frightening.

Narrator 2: Shaking from his whiskers to the tip of his tail, the little mouse managed to stammer his agreement.

Mouse: Where shall I bring the egg when I find one?

Tawb: I live in a hole next to the big oak tree. I will be waiting there for you to bring me an egg. If you don't show up, I shall find you and eat you. And I will eat all of the mice in the forest as well. So mind well and do not fail.

Narrator 1: Terrified, the little mouse went straightaway to find an egg. Soon, he could be seen struggling down the path where he had met old Tawb.

Narrator 2: He grunted as he hauled a pale blue robin's egg toward the old oak tree. The weight of the egg was heavy for his little body, and he was exhausted as he approached the hole.

Mouse: Mr. Snake, I have kept my promise. Here is your egg.

Tawb: Bring it to me, and then you may go on your way.

Narrator 1: Screwing up all his courage, the mouse pushed the egg into the dim entryway. Tawb was waiting with his mouth opened wide. In the darkness, the poor mouse stumbled into the trap. The egg and he went down in one gulp.

Narrator 2: The next day, Abner could see from his perch in the oak tree that the snake was very well pleased with his little trick. The satisfaction on Tawb's face was evident as he emerged from his hole. He was clearly delighted at having fooled the hapless mouse.

 Building Fluency • EMC 3345 • © Evan-Moor Corp.

Tawb: Clever me. I tricked that silly mouse into walking right into my mouth. And I made him bring me an egg in the bargain! Clever, clever me!

Narrator 1: Abner had no doubt at all that Tawb intended to try his trick again. Indeed, before an hour had passed, a chubby gray mouse came scurrying down the forest path.

Narrator 2: Just as he had done before, Tawb grew still in the tall grass and waited.

Narrator 1: And just as he had done before, Tawb waylaid the mouse.

Tawb: Bring me an egg, or I will eat you. And heed my words. If you fail, I shall eat you and all the mice in the forest as well!

Narrator 2: Away went the mouse on his fateful errand. Abner, watching from his perch, decided to take action. Thinking quickly, he came up with a plan. He flew to the riverbank to fetch a small stone. He found a pebble that was just the size and shape of a bird's egg. Picking it up in his beak, he zoomed quickly back to the oak tree. He wanted to be sure that he got back to Tawb's den before the mouse returned.

Narrator 1: Within minutes, Abner saw the mouse approaching, stumbling slowly along the path pushing a speckled egg in front of him. Abner wasted no time. Quickly, he intercepted the mouse and told him to run for his life. Then, he swooped gently to the ground and crept stealthily to the snake's hole.

Abner: Mr. Snake, I've got your egg.

Tawb: Bring it down the hole to me, and then you may go on your way.

Narrator 2: Abner waited a few seconds, just long enough to be sure that Tawb had opened his jaws nice and wide. Then, he dropped the pebble.

Narrator 1: Tawb knew immediately that something was amiss. This egg did not have a pleasant taste or a slick, smooth shell. It was not followed by the wonderful sensation of soft fur sliding down his gullet. Instead, this was a harsh and painful meal to swallow. It seemed to grate at him all the way down his esophagus.

Narrator 2: Just as he was beginning to realize that something was terribly wrong indeed, Tawb heard a voice just outside his burrow's entrance.

Abner: I saw what you did to that mouse yesterday, Tawb, and I didn't think it was nice.

Tawb: Why, it's that meddling crow! What have you done to me?

Abner: I have tried to teach you a lesson, Tawb. Normally, I am not the type to get involved in the affairs of others. But when I see such dastardly actions as yours, I feel compelled to put a stop to them. I hope this is the last we'll see of such tricky and dishonest doings on your part. And just remember this: The next stone I drop will be a good deal bigger!

Narrator 1: With that, Abner flapped his strong black wings and rose gracefully to the top of the oak tree.

Narrator 2: And Tawb slithered miserably down into the deepest part of his den where he passed a long and rather uncomfortable afternoon.

Building Fluency • EMC 3345 • © Evan-Moor Corp.